# DIG AND DISCOVER
# AGATE

by Nancy Dickmann

**CAPSTONE PRESS**
a capstone imprint

T0025430

Published by Capstone Press, an imprint of Capstone
1710 Roe Crest Drive, North Mankato, Minnesota 56003
capstonepub.com

Library of Congress Cataloging-in-Publication Data is available on the Library of
Congress website
ISBN: 9781666342383 (hardcover)
ISBN: 9781666342406 (paperback)
ISBN: 9781666342413 (ebook PDF)

Summary: Agates are rocks with unique patterns of color. Uncover how agates form
from volcanic eruptions and where to search for them.

All internet sites appearing in back matter were available and accurate when this
book was sent to press.

**DISCLAIMER:**

This book provides information about various types of rocks and where and how to find them. Before
entering any area in search of rocks, make sure that the area is open to the public or that you have secured
permission from the property owner to go there. Also, take care not to damage any property, and do not
remove any rocks from the area unless you have permission to do so.

Rock hunting in riverbeds, quarries, mines, and some of the other areas identified in this book can be
inherently risky. You should not engage in any of these activities without parental supervision. Also, you
should always wear proper safety equipment and know how to use any tools that you bring with you. You
should not engage in any activity that is beyond your ability or skill or comfort level. Failure to follow
these guidelines may result in damage to property or serious injury or death to you or others, and may
also result in substantial civil or criminal liability.

The publisher and the author shall not be liable for any damages allegedly arising from the information
in this book, and they specifically disclaim any liability from the use or application of any of the contents
of this book.

Printed and bound in the USA. 4882

# CONTENTS

Words in **bold** are in the glossary.

# INTRODUCTION
## READY TO ROCK

Imagine you're walking along a rocky shoreline. You keep your eyes on the ground. Then you notice a stone shining in the sun. You pick it up for a closer look.

The rock feels a bit heavy. When you rinse it in water, you can see the light shining through it. Looking closely, you see bands of different colors. It's an agate! For a **rock hound**, this is an exciting find. You make a note about it in your notebook.

Agates are found all over the world. People collect them as a hobby. You can collect agates too!

It can take time and focus to find an unpolished agate.

# CHAPTER 1
# WHAT IS AN AGATE?

Agate is a type of **mineral**. A mineral is a solid substance that forms naturally on Earth. Minerals are not alive. They are not made from matter that was once living. Each mineral is made from a mixture of **elements**. Rocks are made up of minerals. A single rock might have several different minerals in it.

Agate belongs to the quartz family. Quartz is made of the elements silicon and oxygen. It forms **crystals**. Some types of quartz make large crystals. But agate crystals are very small. You need a tool called a microscope to see them!

Agate is **translucent**. This means light can pass through it. Agates range in hardness from 6.5 to 7 on the Mohs hardness scale. This scale of 1 to 10 measures how hard minerals are from softest to hardest

Light can shine through thin pieces of agate.

Flashes of color glow from fire agates when light shines on them.

## Types of Agates

Agates come in many types. Most have beautiful bands of color. The bands fit neatly inside each other. The agates you find might not always have complete loops. They could be pieces of a larger stone.

Banded agate is a very common type. It has layers of colors. The layers are all about the same width. In lace agate, the bands have swirls and loops. They look like fancy lace. Fire agate has tiny pieces of minerals that make the agate shimmer with a rainbow of colors.

Moss agates may not have obvious bands.
They have flecks of other minerals trapped inside.
Sometimes these patterns look like leaves or moss.

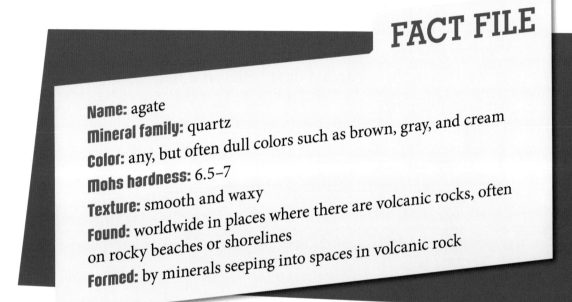

## FACT FILE

**Name:** agate
**Mineral family:** quartz
**Color:** any, but often dull colors such as brown, gray, and cream
**Mohs hardness:** 6.5–7
**Texture:** smooth and waxy
**Found:** worldwide in places where there are volcanic rocks, often on rocky beaches or shorelines
**Formed:** by minerals seeping into spaces in volcanic rock

## FACT

Achates is the ancient name for a river on the island of Sicily in Italy. The ancient Greeks searched for agates along its banks. That's where the stone's name comes from.

# Beautiful Stones

People have collected and used agates for thousands of years. In ancient times, people used agates to make beads and jewelry. They also carved pictures on them. Many people thought agate had magical powers. They thought wearing it could protect them from harm. Some believed it had healing abilities.

Some people make polished agates into beads for jewelry today.

# Fantastic Find!

In 2020, a rock hunter in Soledade, Brazil, found what looked like a normal agate. But when it was split open, there was a surprise inside. The blue and white bands formed a smiling face and googly eyes. The agate looked just like Cookie Monster from the *Sesame Street* TV series!

In the 1800s, Queen Victoria of the United Kingdom often visited Scotland. She wore jewelry made from local agate. This started a trend. People wanted to dress like the queen. Agate jewelry became very popular in the United Kingdom.

# CHAPTER 2
# HOW AGATES FORM

*Whoosh*! Many agates start with a volcano's eruption. When a volcano erupts, it spews out gas and **lava**. Lava is melted, or molten, rock. Bubbles of gas get trapped inside. The lava slowly cools and hardens. It turns into solid rock. The gas bubbles create hollow spaces in the rock. These spaces are like the holes in Swiss cheese!

Much later, water seeps down through the rock. Some of it ends up in the hollow spaces. **Silica** is **dissolved** in water. The water continues to seep downward. But the silica gets left behind. It hardens into tiny crystals. They form thin layers around the insides of the spaces.

This process happens over and over. New layers form inside the old ones. It can take tens of millions of years to fill a space in a rock.

Hot lava can run quickly down a volcano's sides. Agates form after hot lava cools.

# Sedimentary Rock

Some agates form in other kinds of rock. These rocks are made from layers of dirt. The layers also include dead plants and animals. The remains get trapped as the layers of dirt build up. Over time, the layers get squeezed. They turn into rock. But the remains rot away. They leave hollow spaces behind. These spaces fill with silica.

# Agate Colors

The water that forms agates has minerals besides silica. These create an agate's colored bands. Different minerals make different colors. Each layer of an agate forms at a different time. The minerals in the water change over time. Tan and red-brown are common colors.

## FACT

Have you ever seen hot pink agates? What about bright blue ones? People probably dyed them. Brightly dyed agates are popular. Many people buy and collect them.

Agates come in many colors, but some are more common than others.

# CHAPTER 3
# AGATE TREASURE HUNT

Would you like to find your own agates? Hunting for rocks is a popular hobby. You just need to know where to look!

Agates are found anywhere there is volcanic rock. Rocky beaches are the best places to look. The waves constantly bring new rocks to the shore. They also make the stones rounded and shiny. This makes agates easier to spot. Riverbanks and streams often have agates too.

In the United States, ocean beaches in the Pacific Northwest are good places to look. Lakeshores, including along the Great Lakes, have many agates too. Agates from Lake Superior are often red or orange. The deserts of the southwestern United States have fire agates. A gravel road may even include a few agates!

Rocky beaches may have agates.

# Fantastic Find!

In 1905, Austin Mires was rock hunting in Ellensburg, Washington. He found a beautiful blue stone. This kind of stone is now called Ellensburg blue agate. It is found only in the area around Ellensburg. This makes it rare and valuable.

# Stay Safe

Hunting for rocks is fun, but it's important to stay safe. Always rock hunt with an adult. Make sure to tell someone where you are going and when you'll return. Check the tide schedule before visiting a beach. Always stay away from cliffs or drop-offs, and avoid going into caves, mines, or bodies of water.

Some items can be handy and help keep you safe. Bring a cell phone. You should also have water, snacks, and sunscreen. Take a first aid kit. Bring a bucket to hold your finds. Egg cartons are also good. You can label each section with where you found the rock.

## FACT

Workers in the German town of Idar-Oberstein have been known as talented stonecutters for hundreds of years. In the past, they made agate beads. Their beads were traded around the world.

**REMOVAL OF ROCKS OR FOSSILS STRICTLY PROHIBITED**

Always follow the rules on signs posted at your rock hunting site.

## Know the Rules

Where will you hunt for agates? If it's private land, you need permission from the owner. Some parks allow rock collecting. In other places, you can't take rocks home. Make sure to check the rules before you go.

# Spotting Agates

As long as it's not too snowy, winter is a good time to look for agates. Beaches are less crowded than they are in summer. There are often storms that move the sand and gravel around. This might bring agates to the surface.

If you look carefully, you may find an agate among many other types of rocks.

## FACT

Agates sometimes form as **geodes**. These rocks look ordinary on the outside. But the inside is a different story! They have layers of agate bands and a hollow center filled with crystals.

As you explore a beach, keep your eyes on the rocks. Walk with the sun behind you. Remember that agates are translucent. If the sun hits them just right, they will stand out. Try to rock hunt in the morning or late afternoon, when the sun is lower. This can help you see agates.

You've found an interesting rock! But is it an agate? See if the smooth places feel waxy. Hold it up to the light. Does the light pass through? If the rock is dry, rinse it with water. This will make any colored bands show up better.

# CHAPTER 4
# CLEANING AND POLISHING

You've returned with a full bucket. Are there any rocks you're not sure are agates? An adult can use a geology hammer and chisel to split them open. Then you can look for colored bands.

At first, your agates probably won't look like the ones you've seen in pictures. They will be dull and rough. It's time to put on your gloves, dust mask, and safety goggles. Then you can get the agates to look their best!

First, clean your rocks. Soak them in a bucket of hot, soapy water. Then use an old toothbrush to clear away grit and dirt. Keep scrubbing until the rocks are clean.

Polishing an agate helps bring
out its colors and patterns.

Then get a piece of coarse sandpaper and start
sanding. This will smooth the rough edges. Keep the
stone wet as you sand by dipping it in water. Then
switch to finer sandpaper. Keep moving to finer and
finer sandpaper until you get the look you want.

It can take several weeks for a rock tumbler to smooth the rocks.

## Hard Work

Agates are harder than many other stones. Sanding them takes a lot of effort and patience. If you have a rock tumbler, you can use that instead of sandpaper. A rock tumbler has an electric motor. It tumbles a batch of stones in grit until they become smooth.

Once the stone is sanded, you can polish it. This will make it shiny and glossy. You will need rock polishing powder. Some hardware stores carry it. You can also buy it online. Use a damp denim cloth to rub the powder into the stone. If you like, you can polish the stone with a strip of leather. That will make the stone smooth.

## Fantastic Find!

In 2015, scientists in Greece found a small agate bead. It had been buried in a tomb 3,500 years ago. When they cleaned it, they got a surprise. It had a tiny carving of fighting soldiers on it! Researchers named it the Pylos Combat Agate.

# CHAPTER 5
# BUILDING YOUR COLLECTION

You've sanded and polished your agate. Now it's ready to display! It can become part of a rock collection.

When you collect rocks, make sure to take notes. Where did you find each rock? What type was it? Put each rock in a labeled bag. That way they won't get mixed up. If you have a map of the area where you hunted, you can mark your finds on it.

Serious rock hounds catalog their finds. They record each rock they collect. They write down facts about it. You can make a catalog too! You can use cards or do it on a computer.

# Display Your Collection

You can buy a case to display your rocks. You can also make one yourself! Start with a shoebox or a larger box if needed. You can use cardboard strips to divide the box into compartments. Then pad the sections with cotton balls. This will protect the rocks. Don't forget to label each one! You can show your collection to your family and friends.

## SAMPLE CATALOG CARD

**TYPE OF ROCK:** agate

**WHEN FOUND:** July 28, 2022

**WHERE FOUND:** Grayson's Beach

**COLOR:** bands of white and brown

**TEXTURE:** slightly bumpy

**SHAPE:** oval

**SIZE:** 4 x 2 centimeters

**NOTES:** rock tumbler used

Displays can be as simple or complex as you want.

## Clubs

Joining a rock hunting club is a great way to meet other rock hounds. Members might have useful tips to share. Some clubs arrange rock hunting trips. If there is no club in your area, why not start your own? When you can share your rock hunting hobby with others, you can enjoy it even more!

Agates make a fun addition to any rock collection!

# GLOSSARY

**crystal** (KRI-stul)—a solid substance having a regular pattern, often with many flat surfaces

**dissolve** (di-ZOLV)—to mix completely into a liquid

**element** (EH-luh-muhnt)—a substance that cannot be broken down into simpler substances

**geode** (JEE-ohd)—a rock that is lined on the inside with crystals or other minerals

**lava** (LAH-vuh)—the hot, liquid rock that pours out of a volcano when it erupts

**mineral** (MIN-ur-uhl)—a substance found in nature that is not made by a plant or animal

**rock hound** (ROK HAUND)—someone who looks for and collects rocks as a hobby

**silica** (SIL-uh-kuh)—a common mineral that is a mix of silicon and oxygen

**translucent** (trans-LOO-suhnt)—not fully see-through, but able to let some light pass through